Looking for God in All the Wrong Places?

75 GLIMPSES OF THE NOT-SO-OBVIOUS GOD

JODY SEYMOUR

JUDSON PRESS®   VALLEY FORGE

To Betsy, Abigail, and Amanda

whose obvious love

has allowed me the privilege of seeking

the "not so obvious."

LOOKING FOR GOD IN ALL THE WRONG PLACES?
75 GLIMPSES OF THE NOT-SO-OBVIOUS GOD

Copyright © 1990
Judson Press, Valley Forge, PA 19482-0851

Bible quotations in this volume are from the Revised Standard Version of the Bible, copyrighted 1946, 1952, © 1971, 1973 by the Division of Christian Education of the National Council of the Churches of Christ in the U.S.A., and used by permission.

Library of Congress Cataloging-in-Publication Data

Seymour, Jody, 1947–
    Looking for God in all the wrong places? : 75 glimpses of the not
-so-obvious God / Jody Seymour.
      p.   cm.
    ISBN 0–8170–1161–7
    1. Meditations.   I. Title.
BV4832.2.S49   1990   90–35466
242—dc20   CIP

Contents

Spiritual Issues

Seasons of the Gospel

Christmas

Epiphany

Lent—Easter

Pentecost

Introduction

This is a devotional book written for the person who is not quite sure where God is. These words are an offering to the person who finds that some of the answers given from the past do not seem to bear the weight of the present.

It sounds good to say that God is searching for us, and I believe that to be true. God's searching for us, however, does not always mean that we can "turn up" God like some hidden prize beneath a stone. I have discovered in my search for God that the Almighty is not nearly so obvious as some well-meaning people have led me to believe.

You might be one of those seekers who has been disappointed in God because of this "not-so-obvious" characteristic. Some people have ditched the entire search because God has been found to be so unlike their expectations.

I ditched my search for God once, but my Creator did not cease searching for me. I ended up bumping into God in surprising places—places where I was not expecting to find God.

There is an ordinary quality to this Holy One we approach with fear and trembling. The direction and movement of the Christian story is one of the Holy Other becoming ordinary. If we believe this "direction" to be the movement of God, then it is not surprising that what we may discover is a not-so-obvious God who is made manifest in between the sometimes ordinary stuff of life.

What follows is a sharing of my search for the not-so-obvious God. I have included suggested Scripture at the beginning of most selections to allow the reader an opportunity to aid in his or her search.

God is not smaller than our perceptions or expectations but larger than they are. That vastness can make us feel awfully small. We can get lost along the way. We must be ever ready and open to encounter the not-so-obvious God in all sorts of people and places.

The Not-So-Obvious God

In the days of childhood, simple were the thoughts of
    you,
But childish patterns too soon became ripples of
    unfolding mystery.

Still I hear the language of past days echoing that you
    are the same,
But to me you are not the same angelic presence that
    sheltered the child.

Now you are not so obvious,
    for you are an illusive, sometimes distant reality.

I long to see your face as would a child peering into
    clouds hoping to see figures,
But I know the shaping is my own doing
    and then the clouds are gone.

In the mirror I see the child fading daily,
    yet still wanting to see the unseen;
    To make the not so obvious, obvious
        and to hold to certainty's edge
        so as not to grasp at clouds.

Though the angel's touch seems a childish memory
        whose picture is hung upon some wall,
Still I sense the presence of a not-so-obvious God
    who refuses to shout the word I long to hear
        but who whispers even as the thunder reshapes
        the clouds.

Moments in God's Time

God's time is not ours, yet we are in God's time. One way to encounter God is through our imagination. Since God is mostly incomprehensible, our imagination can help us grasp who God is. These selections are imaginative exercises as I try to fathom some very special "moments in God's time."

Dirty Hands

What-ya thinking about, Lord,
When you see this ole ball of clay a-spinning so fast?
We've speeded things up since the day you shaped us
    like a child would mud pies.
We've done some shaping of our own, haven't we,
    Lord?

Are you proud, or do you wonder,
As you hold your head between those tired hands and
    peer at us in wonderment,
If perhaps you didn't make a cosmic slip-up?
Do you notice that the mud is now dried on those
    hands that started it all?
Is it too late to shape us again?

Ah, but you are not a child, are you, Lord?
You've still got something in mind for us.
Are you walking toward us
  Having dipped your hands in that trough which is
    filled with that mysterious water
So that your hands are dripping with the moisture of
    some new creation?

Spinning so fast, aren't we, Lord,
As you reach to us once again.
No mud pie are we in your vision;
Quite dirty, but then you knew that in the beginning,
When you rolled all the stuff around in your hands.

What do you have in mind, One with the mud still on
    your hands?

Our ball of clay has become so out of shape;
   we spin so fast.
Touch us gently once again, O Lord.
Help us feel the hands, the mud . . . the love.

The Morning After

Now he makes me eat dust because I gave them the chance to walk with their faces to the sun. He wanted them to rest in the shade of the tree but not eat its fruit. He was afraid of what they might become if they tasted such possibility.

He is a jealous God, thinking that he should be the only one. He lives in fear for his creatures, so much so that he now takes from me my ability to move easily about the garden. Now I must crawl. But I will remember what he has done.

I heard him weeping like a hurt child as he locked the gate and sent them away. I could hear the sounds of his creatures blaming each other and him. He did not see me follow them, for I have other things to say. As they kick the dust in anger, I shall be there, offering wisdom they can no longer gain from trees.

He does not know what he has done. He was too afraid to let them be like him. Now I will offer them ways to be like me. It is lonely in the dust.

Ah, her promised pain is but a season away. I shall offer her names for the fruits of her pain: Cain and Abel . . . earthy, dusty names.

Holy Moses!

"Get your face out of the dirt, for crying out loud!"

Moses slowly lifted his eyes toward the flaming bush.

"Take off your shoes and show some respect, but for heaven's sake show me your face. We've got business to care for."

"Is that you, God?" Moses spoke quietly, feeling rather foolish conversing with a bush.

"Who do you think it is, Moses? How many other shrubs have called out to you lately?"

"Well, I mean, God, uh . . . is that what I call you? Uh, I really do not know what I am saying."

"Calm down, Moses. You've got the right to be shaken up. You are supposed to be a little confused. I do not do this kind of thing very often."

Moses stuttered, "I suppose you must want something, otherwise you wouldn't be taking the time to scare me and burn this bush. It is burning, isn't it?"

The bush seemed to glow hotter.

"Sure I want something. Get yourself back to Egypt and tell that rascal Pharaoh to set my people free, and now!"

"But, God, I am a sheep keeper, and besides, as you can tell, I'm not very good with words."

The flame seemed to be frozen in time.

"You're wasting my time and yours, Moses. This is

not some boxwood to whom you are talking! I know what I am doing. Don't worry about the words. If I can make a bush burn and still be green, I can give you some words when needed."

Moses' excuses began melting in the presence of the flame.

"Well, God, pardon me for asking, but when I speak to that bunch of disgruntled slaves, who shall I say has sent me to fetch them? What's your name?"

The silence was awesome, then the bush burned more intensely than before.

"You people of mine, always wanting to name things. Ever since Adam you've had this propensity to name things. You must feel that if you name something, you have control over it. Well, this time it just ain't so."

Moses picked himself up from his knees and turned from the fire. He knew that he could not look back since his direction had been set for him. From over his shoulder he heard a voice one more time:

"Okay, okay . . . Tell them 'I AM' has sent you. Let them chew on that."

As Moses reached the bottom of the mountain, he heard the breeze whisper, "Why do they need to know my name? It is enough that I know theirs."

Lift Up the Sacrifice

He made sure the blade was sharp so that death would come quickly. His shepherd's knowledge would allow him to make death almost painless. He knew which vessels to slash so that for the one sacrificed it would seem like sleep.

But this day it was to be no sheep laid upon the high rock of the mountain. God had asked him for his son, Isaac—the child of laughter, the product of bewildered faith. What kind of God was this who played with a father's heart?

Abraham listened, hoping to hear another voice as he tied Isaac's hands behind his back. His son had asked him earlier why they had not brought a lamb for the sacrificial offering. Now Isaac's lips were still. The question had been answered in the binding of his hands by the one who had taught him in his youth of a God who was harsh, yet loving.

Abraham's wait produced no other voice, only the shrill sound of the wind as it blew upon the rugged face of the mountain. The fledgling father of a vagabond people raised his knife. He could no longer see Isaac for his vision was clouded with tears. He knew that his first pierce with the blade must be exact so as to kill without pain. The sacrifice already accomplished in his bleeding heart, Abraham lowered the knife toward his son.

"Stop. It is enough that you are willing."

It was God's voice, a voice that had before told

Abraham of the laughter of disbelief and the uncertainty of strange lands. He recognized that voice.

As an exhausted father held a weeping Isaac to his chest, he wondered: *What kind of God is it who would offer up an only son to be sacrificed?*

. . . and the wind seemed to whisper, "One day, I shall. . . ."

God's Yes

Gabriel shuffled into the office and threw his horn onto the sofa. He then cast himself across the inviting cushions and laid his tired head beside his somewhat tarnished instrument.

"I'm tired of blowing my brains out on that trumpet. Nobody seems to be paying any attention."

He looked over at the desk where piles of folders were bunched together in a strange sort of order. Behind the mounds of paperwork he could see the boss rubbing his forehead with his fingers as if he were trying to ease the tension from a headache.

"I'm tired of it myself," said the boss. "I've drowned the rascals, knocked over their silly towers, given them clear-cut rules to live by, and even sent my prophets. They are still insistent on whistling their own tunes. They can't hear you or me for their own clatter."

The boss then reeled around in his squeaky chair and reached for a folder that was wrapped securely with a thick rubber band. He peeled off the rubber band and shot it toward Gabriel, laughing to himself as a child. Gabriel jerked his head just in time to have the soft missile land beside him on the sofa.

"What'ya got there, Boss?"

"Oh, it's something I've been saving ever since I opened shop. I've had it in mind all along, but the cost factor is so high that I have been reluctant to make use of it."

He opened the file and gently laid the papers out before him as if he were handling someone else's prize possession. Gabriel found this behavior to be rather peculiar since there was nothing around that was not the boss's doing.

The curious angel leaned forward and tried to see over the stack of papers that partially hid the newly opened file. The boss seemed to be reading. Gabriel noticed the serious expression on his face. He also noticed that the more the boss read, the more he seemed to shake his head ever so slightly, as though he were getting into something he would rather not.

"Is this some kind of new scheme you've concocted to get their attention?" the angel whispered. There was no reply. The boss was staring out the window, looking off into eternity. Gabriel had only seen this kind of expression once before, and he had inquired as to what it meant, only to be told, "Oh, nothing . . . just thinking about something that I may need to do later."

Gabriel upped the volume a bit: "Boss . . . Boss . . . ."

Still he seemed lost to his gaze. Then the angel addressed him in a more formal manner, since this seemed to be getting serious: "God, what are you going to do?"

God turned slowly toward his chief helper and spoke: "I think it's time, Gabriel. He's been wanting to go, you know. I've been too protective, perhaps. But, after all, he is right. His coming will make my intentions perfectly clear. Still . . . I am afraid of the cost."

Gabriel was without words, but God did not seem to be paying much attention to him.

God continued: "I've got the plan all here. We'll have to do it the hard way . . . the real way. It is the only way those stubborn people of mine will be able to understand. He'll have to start out like everybody else. I have this young girl in mind, but you'll have to go and try to explain it to her. That husband-to-be of hers will just have to go along with the plan . . ."

Gabriel was confused. He had learned, however, not to expect to understand all of the things that came from behind this desk.

"Okay, Gabriel, go get him. He's been wanting to to do this for a long time, and I've been holding back. Go find that boy of mine and tell him I said yes."

Dreams Come True

He could do anything. In one moment he was the captain of a huge ship. In another moment he could be master of his feelings as he winked at the young girls in the village where he commanded much respect. But all of this was in his dreams, for in reality he owned no ship, and he was unable to even look the young girls in the face. He was only free in his dreams. Awake he was shy and afraid.

On some evenings he longed for sleep. It was then that he could discover again some new strength that lay dormant inside of him.

But on this evening he could not sleep. Reality stood at the gate and would not let him pass to the place of rest from whence some mystical answer might come. At last he had been able to look a young girl in the face—not in some dream, but with his eyes fully open as he gazed upon hers.

Now he wished that what was real was a dream. Her announcement had shattered the fragile strength he had gained over the past weeks. His hands had always been strong in shaping the wood, but dealing with people was different. At last he had found a person who was gently able to pull from him that dormant ability to lift his face and be himself—awake.

Tears filled his eyes, allowing the blessed gift to finally come. Sleep cradled him as a quiet benediction to a pain-filled day. Quickly his dream came this night. There was no waiting. The brightness of the light almost woke him.

And then the voice:

> Let your fear sleep, for the one who is to be yours can still be. When you awaken, look again into her face and you will see that never again do you have to lower your eyes. The child is mine, Joseph. I am giving him to her, to you, and to all the world. When you awaken, you will be strong. You will call our son Jesus, for he will save his people.

Joseph woke early. The rest of Nazareth was still sleeping. He ran like a child, like the captain of a new ship, like one who was the master of his feelings. He ran to Mary's house.

One Dark Night

What was the point in going on? His wife had died two months before, leaving him alone to face the empty nights. His children had moved away and seemed only to return home out of duty. He looked out the window and saw that the streets, which had earlier been crowded and noisy, were now still and dark.

He walked downstairs, passing all kinds of people who were now sleeping after their long journeys. The recent increase in taxation had required them to make the same pilgrimage he had made.

As he walked behind the inn, his thoughts centered upon taking his life. It was, of course, against his faith, but his religion seemed to him now like some of the dried herbs that his wife used to hang beside the window. The freshness of his faith had faded. No dried fragment from the past would add any flavor to his bland life.

As he looked down toward the trough where a cow was preparing to drink, he noticed the reflection of an exceptionally bright star. He turned to see its light first-hand. It was then that he noticed a woman sleeping in the hay beside the cow. A man was standing nearby in the entrance of a cave that seemed to be used as a kind of stable. The man was holding something in his arms.

A sound came from the bundle that the man was holding. With the heaviness of his life still weighing him down, he walked over to the man, who was holding a baby, of all things. He looked into the man's eyes, then down to the face of the child.

"What a world for a child to be born into!" he said with the same spirit of sadness that had accompanied him on his walk from the inn.

The young father peered back at him and simply said, "The world will be different now."

As he walked back toward the inn, the lonely man felt his despondency lift and noticed again how bright was the star.

The Edge of the Wilderness

He was tired, and this was just the beginning.
There were too many voices echoing in his mind.
There was the gentle whisper of familiarity that called
him to go back home to security and to the love of
his family. Was he not expected, after all, to follow in
his father's trade? He was needed.

Then there was the stirring within him that came
from seeing the hope and despair on the faces of his
own people—people who had waited too long. There
was much to do and many roads ahead from which to
choose. Which way should he go?

He rested on a large rock that easily could have
been an altar of sacrifice, for this was what he felt. It
was as if there were nothing left of him after his
struggle in the desert. Each evening as the burning
sun had set, he had rested in any shade available. He
felt as if he were falling from the very pinnacle of the
temple. His flesh burned as though it had been torn
by the sharp edges of the earth that seemed to await
his sacrifice.

Now at the edge of his wilderness, he could barely
remember the cool water that had surrounded him
but a few days before. He tried to see again the
vision of a bird's shadow coming over him as he felt
wet with acceptance. He had been so sure then,
before the wilderness.

He lifted himself up from the rock, for this was no
time for a sacrifice. He filled his chest with the dry air

of his homeland—a land that offered both life and death. He remembered that this was the day when his childhood friend was to be married in Canaan.

He would go. What madness—a voice urging him to go to a wedding at such a time. Was it appropriate to go and make merry with friends at this ritual of new beginnings?

He walked expectantly toward the road that led to Canaan as he whispered to himself and the wilderness, "O Father, what on earth could I possibly do for you and your people at a wedding?"

He heard no answer.

Salvation

"Most of them are fools. They are easily led by anyone who makes promises. I take their money easily, for they do not possess the courage to rise up and change the powers that control their lives. They think of me as dirty because I sacrifice a few principles. Let them remain 'clean' and stupid.

"Who is the one they clamor after this time? I would at least like to look on his face to see what kind of person it is who is able to give them even false hope. I know they will not let me pass. The only power they have over the likes of me is when they are together like this as a sea of people.

"I will not be stopped by this rabble. I have climbed over people all my life; surely I can climb high enough to get a good look at him in spite of the persistent throng who would try to deny me.

"What? How is it that he knows my name? Look at their faces. They cannot believe that it is I whom he calls to come down from my lofty place. Again I have them in my grasp.

"But why me? What is it that he wants? Will he require something of me? Perhaps I should ignore his call to me.

"But how did he know my name?"

And Zacchaeus climbed down.

Transfigured

In time's mirror, distant figures are seen talking to
    him,
Reflections of the past made present,
    foreshadowing a cloudy future and a cross.

His face shines as he speaks with one whose brows
    were singed by a burning bush.
And he smiles as he hears Elijah recount the hardness
    of Israel's heart.

Then from the cloud comes the thunder of a voice
    not man's.
And the One who sifts time between his fingers like
    so much sand speaks:

"This is my beloved Son . . . listen to him."
And confused disciples are told to keep the vision
    locked in their hearts
until his tomb is unlocked by the thunder.

Down the mountain they are led,
    their lives singed by the nearness of a power who
    plays with time.
And they see this Son of Thunder reach toward the
    demons
    as time pushes them toward a valley and a cross.

Stones on the Ground

Through her tears she traced the memory of a father who somehow never noticed she was there. She relived those first fragile relationships with the young boys in the village. She remembered how she had longed for someone to hold her in a special way. No one ever had.

She had reached out to many, hoping to find the one. She had given most of herself away. The limp figure that the religious leaders dragged down the crowded streets this sultry afternoon was empty of most feelings. Little was left inside of her with which to feel.

At last she had been found out. It was almost a relief. She had been convicting herself for years. She had found herself guilty even in those days of childhood when her father seemed to see no innocence in her eager face.

Now she was condemned, cast at the feet of some religious teacher who was to pronounce the required sentence of death. It was the law. The adultery was clear.

In her stooped position, all she saw was a pair of feet in the dust. There came a hand down to her face. She drew back in preparation for the blow, but the hand, instead, only drew a few lines in the loose sand beside her.

Something was said, but she was no longer listening. It mattered not.

Then she heard the silence. What was this silence
that filled the place with sudden peace?

A hand touched her face gently. Never had she
been touched in such a way. The feeling in the hand
was the kind she had longed for from her father.

Looking up into the face, she heard his words break
the silence. It was only then that she noticed that the
crowd was gone.

"Does anyone now condemn you?"

And then with a sort of smile, "Rise . . . go . . .
and sin no more."

He turned and walked away. As she rose to her
feet, she saw the many stones that lay upon the
ground.

Why the Weeping?

They saw tears in his eyes as he stood alone on the hill overlooking the city. His moist vision frightened them, for he was their strength. What did these sudden tears mean? Were not tears a sign of weakness, of defeat?

Peter turned toward the whispers, "Shut up and at least leave him alone with his thoughts."

Peter's words made him appear to be strong, but he, too, was afraid. He sensed that the crowds seemed to have more and more questions on their faces the nearer they came to the city. The longing and the hope were still apparent on the people's faces, but so was the growing anxiety.

Andrew and John built a fire which the others huddled around in silence. Jesus was still standing alone on the rock that seemed to hang over the glowing lanterns of Jerusalem.

"I'm worried about him. He seems to be getting depressed or something."

"How would you know, Judas?" shouted Matthew. "Your level of sensitivity was evident the other evening when you criticized him for allowing that woman to anoint his feet."

Judas stared indignantly at his fellow disciple and said no more. They were all edgy. Was it because they were drawing near to Jerusalem? Was it because of the tears of their leader as he looked solemnly at the city?

All of them shared the memory of Jesus' earlier words on the journey: "O Jerusalem, Jerusalem, killing the prophets and stoning those who are sent to you."

Did Jesus remember his previous words this particular evening as he viewed the city from a distant hill? Why the tears? What would happen in Jerusalem?

Judas felt a hand on his shoulder. He turned and looked into Jesus' eyes—eyes no longer filled with the dampness of sorrow. Jesus' words seemed to mingle with the crackling of the fire: "Though you are filled with fear, did you notice how beautiful were the lilies in the setting sun?"

And Judas wondered, *How could he think of flowers?*

A Passing Parade

He held tightly to his father's head so that he could keep his balance.

"Watch it, son, you're going to blind me with your fingers."

The young lad eased his grip, feeling more secure now that his father held him tightly about the ankles. The view from atop his father's shoulders was spectacular.

"Here he comes, Dad! Here he comes!"

He could see the center of attention smiling and gently nodding toward the shouts of the crowd. He appeared and then disappeared as the colt upon which he rode moved forward in an uneven cadence. Between the raised hands of the crowd, the child's vision of the man was sporadic.

"Get me closer, Dad. I want to see him up close."

The father pushed his way through the teeming crowd and stepped awkwardly on the edge of some palm branches that had been thrown in the roadway.

It was perfect timing, for just as the boy and his father made their way to the front of the crowd, the man on the colt approached. His strong eyes suddenly caught the boy's eyes in their grasp.

The boy reached toward the man and caught his outstretched hand. For a moment the procession stopped and these two individuals shared a smile. Then the man was gone, pulled forward by the tide of enthusiasm.

The father lowered his son from his shoulders.
They walked away from the noise that was soon at a
distance.

"Dad, did you see the way he looked at me . . .
and the way he smiled? It was the way Grandpa used
to hold my hand and smile before he died. Is this
man going to die, too, Dad?"

"No, no, son. This Jesus is young and full of life
and hope. Just listen to all the people shouting. This is
just the beginning."

Father and son walked toward home. The boy
could not let go of the mysterious feeling that had
stirred inside of him when he held to the hand of the
stranger from Galilee.

Mary's Lament

Soft still is his torn flesh;
  soft like this grave cloth.
His head against my breast reminds me of the night
    of his birth;
There again I wrapped him in gentle clothes.

  He is alone now, his cross vacant,
    just as on that night of his birth we were alone,
    A solitary scene framed by animals and confused
      shepherds.

  His hands grow cold;
    His wounds are painted with dried life.
So soon it seems, he was warm with the pain of my
    labor still cradling him.

  I saved the myrrh, my son, and one of the cloths of
    your birth.
Now the spice and the cloth hold you again,
  But I shall not.

  They have taken you from me,
    surprisingly, like you were given.
But I should not be surprised,
    for even that first night as I held you,
      I was afraid for you.

  Hold him gently, linen of death,
    even as I held him before life,
      softly in my womb.
There in my sheltering darkness he waited for life.
  Now he waits again.

O God, his life came to me so unexpectedly.
Now look at our son so lifeless.
  Was his hope for new life one of his many dreams?
So many were his childhood fantasies.

What can you do with death,
  O One who stunned me so with life?
See how still he is, so unlike he was
  when I first felt him move within me.

Hard to Love

"I get tired of them claiming that I am on their side no matter what the cause!"

"But, Father, you must be used to that by now. They've been doing it for thousands of years."

God walked over to a moss-covered rock, eased himself down onto its cool, inviting surface, put his head between his hands, and looked out over eternity.

"They seem unable to understand even now. Don't they, Father?"

Jesus put his arm over God's bowed shoulders and stood beside him for moments that knew no measure.

"Sometimes I wonder why I sent you to them, Son. They call my name when it's convenient and go their merry way when faced with the hard part of my ways. They're still selfish children, Jesus!"

Jesus knew that silence was the most appropriate response to such remarks. After a while, he stepped to the side of the rock and sat down beside God, leaning slightly toward him to gain his attention.

"It's hard to love them sometimes, isn't it, Father?"

God turned his peering eyes toward his son and reached for his hand, as if to gain help in standing up. In that moment he saw the scars. Holding to his son's hand, he looked up and spoke, this time more gently than before.

"Yes, my Son, sometimes it is."

Issues of Life and Death

Waiting Angels

Winged death, they wait for life;
   still in their cocoons,
      saviors of peace they become.
But what is this peace they offer?

Angels are they, ready to share;
   messengers from a god—
      a deity whose hand is metal,
      whose salvation promises fire and death.

"Trust me," they whisper and, "make me more in my
      waiting;
Your enemy is visited too with many angels waiting to speak."

Blind, we see not, for they come from the same god,
   who smiles as we pour our wealth into images like him.

"No other gods . . . no other gods," still echoes from
      the heavens,
But the angels we call missiles have no ears to hear the cry.

But we who can hear must surely wonder, What is peace?
While angels of death, handmade, grow larger in their
      cocoons.

Do we not think they will one day break forth from
      their waiting
  and give us their birth of death—
      their god's gift of peace?

Seeds of Power

And on the seventh day God rested,
But just before he closed his eyes,
   he gently planted the seeds of power,
      deep within the mystery of creation.

For countless years the seeds lay dormant,
      resting power surrounding Adam's children.
Then one day someone dug up the seed,
   and a mushroom cloud sprouted forth.

Twice the seeds were planted by us;
   returned into the earth God shaped.
And its power reshaped all it touched,
   leaving creation destroyed in its shadow.

Now we stand beneath the cloud,
   awed and afraid by the seeds we've sown.
O God who first planted,
   may we create and not destroy.

The Other Side
of the Mushroom Cloud

I imagined that I was facing the Lord with the shadow of a mushroom-shaped cloud still in my memory. I looked into God's face—a face that had intimately known our world, smelling its flowers and suffering its pain. Into that face I threw my question: "Why did you let it happen?"

Without hesitation and with a touch of anger, God replied, "Why did *you* let it happen?"

God turned and began to walk away from me. I reached out and grasped the flowing garment.

"Where are you going, Lord," I asked in bewilderment.

"I am going to make another world," God responded. "It will take me billions of years to fashion what I want, but time is nothing to me. Look at what you have done to my creation—a creation that I loaned to you. My hand formed it, and now your hand has destroyed it."

"But, Lord," I stammered, "did you not intend to redeem our world?"

"It *was* redeemed, my foolish child. You let it slip through your fingers. I did not choose for you to destroy yourselves with the folly of the unchained atom. I created those atoms that you used as your means of death."

"But, Lord, what could we have done? We needed security from those who would destroy us."

I suddenly realized the foolishness of my petition. Where was my security now?

"What could you have done?" God responded. "You could have fed people instead of building metal gods full of fire. You could have risked your life for Life instead of for Death. You could have chosen the other way."

God then slipped around a star-dust horizon and reached for some fiery mass as a child would a ball of clay.

Distant Chernobyl

So much distance between us;
   the more the better, we say.
For we are enemies, yet not at war, we say.

Their names are strange to us,
   their ways veiled in mystery.
So the distance is comfortable, we say.
Then a power beyond us vanquishes the distance.
   Though not at war, we are invaded.
"But do not fear, all is well," they say.

But the smoke fills the air,
   and the winds know no walls nor who the enemy
     is,
And the tragedy created by powers thought tamed
   destroys the distance.
And experts tell our children to drink their milk,
   for it is safe, they say.

As calm assurance fills the air,
   the distance is gone;
For people with strange-sounding names from far
   away are dying
   as we drink our milk, stained with small reminders
   of why they die.

Then smiling faces tell us,
   "Be not afraid of our enemy,
     for our weapons will defend us."

So we drink our milk and wonder,
    for we know the weapons are filled with that which
    stains our drink and slowly kills our enemy with
    strange-sounding names.
"But do not fear; the distance is so far," they say.

Colored Water

"Colored" read the sign above the fountain whose
    water I had drunk.
Would I be sick from drinking "colored" water?
  For I was a "white only,"
    though but a child.

I asked a big person,
  but my mistaken drink was washed away with
    words.
So I waited to see if I would turn ill,
  or perhaps "colored,"
    for no one would say.

There was only laughter at my childish question,
  And the strange word "nigger" tossed about like a
    toy—
    some strange enjoyment I did not understand.

Now I am a "big person" with no signs to read above
    fountains.
And my children laugh when I tell them the colored
    water story,
  For they do not understand how water could make
    people sick.

No Longer Children

Did you pause for a moment, O God,
  as you rested in your easy chair
    and listened to the seven o'clock news?—
    "Artificial heart recipient improves."

Could it be that your children have grown up,
  have answered so many of the questions?
So many needs are now simply wants.
  We have become the creators.

"Test-tube baby celebrates birthday."
  You turn down the volume for you have heard
    much this day—
    matters of the heart, both flesh and plastic.

Satellites tell us of cloud and sunshine.
  From the heavens we plot our future,
    a lofty vision, once held by you alone.
Our heads are full of knowledge; we are no longer children.

You turn from our broadcast—not news to you—
  and walk slowly to the potter's wheel,
    that ancient, turning pedestal of creation.
Earth beneath your nails, you shape again.

You know that in the dark we are children still.
  That beating in our chest, though lovingly tampered with,
    begins and ends in you.
Perhaps we too should turn down the volume
  and hear the turning of the wheel.

Laughter in the Darkness

Life sometimes laughs at us.
Thirty-four is too young to die.
As the rug is pulled from beneath our feet,
    we fall and hear the laughter in the darkness.

It is a cruel joke of sorts,
    to have life so full and then to have it taken.
We who try so hard to win, are surprised by defeat,
    so we feel alone in the darkness.

It is not fair, and never shall be, to have life jerked
        away.
And so we stammer like a comic before blank
        unfeeling faces,
    and the laughter comes from off-stage.

What have you done to mock us so, God, to tease us
        with life,
    and then to leave us with questions?
What are we to do but shake our heads and our fists
        at the laughter?

But then it was for the laughter that your boy came
        to us.
Behind him in a cloud-filled horizon came the
        laughter surrounding his cross.
Thirty-three was too young to die,
    And the joke seemed on God that Friday.

Into the emptiness they carried Jesus,
and the walls of his tomb echoed with the silent
laughter of death.
Only the stone held its crescendos back.

But God laughs last, for divine love is bigger than the
darkness.
God simply walked into the tomb and picked up
death as though it were an overused joke, and
smiled . . .
And God and Jesus walked out into the early morning
sun and laughed.

A Second Death—Born Again

You made us play God, Karen,
   like children playing tag with death.
We ran across the grass barefoot,
   to wonder, afraid to be touched.
     And you waited.

Some strange encounter with fun caused you to sleep.
But there was no prince to end the tale,
   to touch your lips and break the spell of time.

You slipped slowly back to childhood,
   held by the shadowy mystery of machines—
     princes of our minds but without the magic to
     make you smile again.
     And you waited.

And so the joust began to set you free,
   free from the clinging arms of plastic life.
And our moist vision saw no victory for anyone who
     fought the battle.
     And we waited.

Then the muted trumpet sounded its triumph,
   and the "princes of our minds" were banished.
   But you did not leave; nor did you smile.
For you lived in a land beyond our touch and theirs.

The sands in the glass spilled over and over.
Time for those who loved you hung heavy,
   like the morning fog that would not lift.

But like a child expecting birth,
    you waited.

Then one day, unexpectedly, a prince came and ran
        across the grass and touched you.
The game was suddenly over.
Birth a second time came to you;
    a second death to give you life.

Sarah

(Written for friends in memory of their daughter)

Sarah, you were but a whisper as we waited for the
 crescendo.
There was so much we wanted to say,
 but into the silence we only spoke your name.

But there is One who knows you, Sarah;
 One who understands your incompleteness,
  for we who waited do not.
He is the One who hears our whispers and our tears;
 And you are his now, Sarah.

Our emptiness for all that could have been rattles
 around in us
 and all is noise.
So we barely hear the whisper,
 and we hurt to hold you as he now does.

But in the noise he hears your name.
And now he whispers it to you, so you know.
He speaks our words for us,
 and you know how much you were loved,
  as now Love holds you.

You shall grow up in that love, Sarah,
For our God is one who speaks above the noise and
 shapes from what is broken
 a new creation amidst birth's mystery.

O Sarah, God our Father and our Mother holds you.
Birth is understood by She who carried us and all
 creation in the womb caressed by stars.

So we whisper your name to the night sky,
    and know that it is heard.

Skeptical as we are, Sarah,
    we who glimpse distant angels only in books, now
    are believers,
    for an angel now you are;
        Our child, now God's.

O Mother of all that is, hold us, even as you hold
    Sarah,
For we are lost amidst noisy questions.
Speak to us in your silent language of loving creation;
And in the stillness we shall whisper your name and
    hers.

Wounded Sister

(A poem written after hearing of the suicide of the "Singing Nun")

Your songs were chords of innocence
  wrapped gently around years too simple.
There were no protests in your words,
  no anger to stir the conscience.
  Perhaps you sang as does a bird,
    simply because that was who you were.
There was no need to make a statement;
  your melody betrayed your naiveté . . .
    and ours.
  Before the days of Vietnam and the nights of
      Watergate,
    on the very eve of the fall of Camelot,
You gave to us your simple song of life,
  and we hummed the tune without thinking.
  Where did the journey turn suddenly for you,
    as you found yourself singing with no music?
O bride of Christ, did your marriage fail you?
O wounded sister, did your brothers not sing with
      you?
  Did you nervously turn the ring on your finger
    as you tried to compose other songs?
Could your soul hear the words amidst the noise of
    electric guitars and synthesizers?
  Did we, your listeners, fail you, our sister?
Were we passengers on a train as it passed you by
      one evening
    as you tried to sing your song alone in the station?
  O Father, listen well to the song of our wounded
      sister now gone from us.

O husband Christ, speak to her of things
   she could not bear to sing about.
  Your shattered vows, your tarnished ring,
   judge each of us who once listened;
For there are so many songs we do not hear,
   rhythms of wounded hearts lost in the noise.
  You remain our sister; your song is your witness.
And we hear its all-too-simple melody as we try to
   sing and make sense of the notes.
  For we too are wounded as we try to carry a tune
   beside the noise of passing trains.

Frozen Flowers

Nursing homes are a crisis of faith. As I walk down the halls and see face after face of palsied emptiness, I long to turn the corner and grab some fleeing angel that I might wrestle with God.

Tongues hanging limply from pale lips, the smell of the constant swamp of urine, and feeding tubes are an embarrassment to a God who is supposed to care. "God Almighty" are the frozen words from the woman with fearful eyes who cannot remember why she pulled herself out of the chair to walk to the door.

I feel weak when I escape from those halls filled with the odor of decaying life. I want to stand beneath some waterfall and rinse myself clean from what is. "Why" is too small a word to describe the fear and loneliness that clings to the flowery wallpaper in the rooms—flowers that will never smell sweet like hope.

Come wrestle with me, God, while I can still remember why I pull myself from the chair. Let me scrape and claw my sweaty body alongside yours in anger and longing. And as I lay defeated and disjointed upon the earth of your making, whisper your name to me as you leave. Promise me and those blank stares of your withered children, that someday the flowers on the wall will quiver in the wind and life will be made fresh. Promise me that even while I see the vacancy within their lives, that there are countless rooms waiting to be furnished in a house not made with hands.

Let me catch the angel while my legs will run. Let me at least know as I wrestle with the emptiness that you hold even that emptiness in your hands. Help me still believe, even as I see those frozen flowers and hold your withered children.

Spiritual Issues

Turn Around

I looked over my shoulder;
   the year had its back to me.
I reached for it, but it was just beyond my grasp.
I wanted to ask it questions before it took its leave,
But it seemed that time had its own time for coming and going.

I wanted to plead for one more chance to love.
I wanted to argue for one more opportunity to touch another;
But it took all of my past chances with it to that place,
   a place where the past is stored in cells of distant memory
   only to be brought out to the light at some eternal
      gathering point
   when it will be time for the soul to do its cleaning.

I was angry with the year,
   for though I knew it would leave,
   I erred in my judgment of how much it would take with it.
It left only shadows of what might have been,
   etched in auras of hope's light of what might yet be.

My pleas for the year to return,
   if just for a moment of reflection,
      were lost amidst the noise of parties celebrating its leaving,
      of parties greeting the arrival of the new.
But I was alone with the shadows and the haunting suspicion
   that if some new vision did not come to me,
   the new would resemble the old that left,
      taking so much with it.

Life's mysteries tease the planner with the reality of
    tragedy and death;
While unearned sunsets pass by unnoticed by busy
    time-travelers.
We who travel, lose time, greet time, kill time, beat time,
   but never do we possess time.
Time holds us in its grasp
   and we are the ones who may slip through its fingers
    as sands counted only by God.

Look at me face to face
   and let me ask of you questions
   so that I may this year find that illusory happiness
    that so many travelers seek.

So, I reached out for the year as it came through that
    ever-moving portal.
I tugged on its sleeve to get its attention
   so as to see it face to face.
What I saw frightened me,
   for its face was my own.

There was but a brief, beckoning smile as it turned to
    go its way into a time just beyond my reach.
And the smile seemed to say,
   "Follow . . . it is yours to make;
    you and me . . . the year, new."

High Expectations

"There is nothing new under the sun!" That is what the somewhat cynical preacher said in the book of Ecclesiastes, but then what did he know? He could not have imagined test-tube babies or artificial hearts. He had no vision of microcomputers or space shuttles.

In our hearts, however, we all know what the writer of those ancient words meant. As we face a year that the calendar tells us is new, we often sense that there is nothing new about us. We have tried to change old ways, but the flowing waters of our lives have cut paths and valleys that are too deep. The old year remains with us as wrinkles do on our faces. Cosmetics or apparel only sustain the illusion that there is something new about who we are.

Most of us long to have something new happen to us or in us, but our spirits are pessimistic about the reality of it ever happening. We know who we are, no matter what image we share with others. Is there anything new under the sun about us?

Part of our problem is that we are a people of high expectations. We have been taken in by the myth of progress, which states that for change to be valid, it must be rapid and spectacular. We forget that we are the product of creation. Trees change slowly. The river's path is the product of years of steady movement.

A slight change in human personality is significant. There can be something new about us if we will struggle to possess the serenity to celebrate the little steps we take toward change. New Year's resolutions are often laid aside quickly because we expect to be able to change by leaps and bounds rather than by inches.

The God who knows that the sun rises on a new world every day measures us by inches, not by yards. There can be the new; one small step at a time.

Impatiently

The leaves seem to whisper his name as they quake in
    his presence.
How I long to be moved as they are, but the wind is
    still in my life.

I need the coolness of his spirit reminding me of his
    wonder,
But I see only shoots of life struggling to bloom in
    the desert.

I long to be nursed as a child held fast to its mother's
    breast,
But I am forced to stumble forward as if taking the
    first steps of faith.

What kind of God are you who makes me seek so
    earnestly?
Why can I not be cradled in certainty,
    knowing always your hand is near?

But others have waited and have known the power
    of your ever-moving love.
Impatiently the child within wants to know, to see, to
    feel, to touch.

I yearn to be grown full in understanding,
    but my steps are timid and uncertain.
Yet even in my falling I sense a Father's eyes
    watching his child joyfully, painfully grow up.

Dust's Surrender

The earth's dust surrendered and gave a gentle
    welcome to its friend the rain.
The shy green of the grass lost its timidity and
    shouted its color across the day.

Creation drank deeply of heaven's happy tears,
And flowers danced to songs played by a symphony of
    winds.

Fall gently on my field, rain of heaven.
Surprise the dusty places of my life with your
    showers.
Remind my dry spirit that new life waits just beyond
    dust's surrender.

The Leaves of October

To what unknown place does the wind of February
    blow the leaves of October?
Broken pieces of leftover life,
    forgotten and homeless,
    strays of nature's family.
Swirling about, moved by some unseen power to
    some mysterious rest.
Do such to my broken pieces, O Lord of wind and
    rest.
Hide away my leaves of October that keep me from
    living full days of February.
Let your blowing Spirit cradle the stray portions of
    my life.
Gather them in your place of mystery until the wind
    stirs the green leaves of your spring.

Woven

Unfelt is the weave until the unraveling.
Then a frayed edge shows design,
  a binding mystery holding me together.

Creating hands cast the shuttle, the back and forth
    rhythm of a heart,
  until there comes a pattern never matched again.

Tight sometimes is the weave, unseen threads blended
    before my knowing.
But then there is the tearing that always comes from
    the pull of life.

Mend me, patient Weaver, as you did the spoiled
    clay.
Recast the fabric, for only you know the scheme as
    the threads of mystery both bind and separate.

Tossed from hand to hand is your shuttle,
And somewhere between those hands I am woven.

Baptized Forever

We are gently tossed in a tide of love in our mother's
    womb,
    Knowing only the wetness of acceptance.

Suddenly we are born to life, screaming into a dry
    wilderness;
    A stranger from a salty sea, still damp with love.

But we look back longingly toward the safety of the
    waters,
    Somehow wanting to be unborn in water's calm.

Then a sacred wetness touches us, covering life with
    Life.
    Baptized, we feel the memory of the once-cradling
    sea.

Named and chosen, held by Spirit.
    Again accepted, wet with the blessing of the maker
    of seas;
    Baptized forever.

To Abigail on Confirmation Day

So near it seems—that time I held you lightly in my arms.
You were life for the first time through me;
   Yet I knew you were from beyond my grasp.

Today that Beyond touches you like it did once
      before when sacred waters baptized you,
And God reminded all who witnessed that parents
      were but stewards of precious, shared dust.

So God bends down today and listens well to vows
     spoken now by you,
For it is time for you to claim that One who claimed
     you from those sacred waters.

On this day God remembers another time,
   When God's own child responded to the call,
     And waited from water's edge to hear a heavenly whisper:
     "With you I am well pleased."

Abigail, today the One who gave you to us is pleased
     with what you do,
For you have chosen to struggle with God's ways,
    And today God hears your "yes."

In moments you will feel beyond God's touch,
And when you do, whether it be by choice or
     circumstance,
   remember this your day of confirmation,
    When the Beyond came near and heard your "yes,"
    never to forget it nor you.

Sandblasting Grace

Scatter your tiny pebbles of love across my life, Lord.
Pound me with the force of your powerful gentleness.
Cleanse me from the stains of the past that I wish to
    hide.
Uncover the beauty you created long ago, hidden by
    yesterdays.
Blast me with the wind and the sand of your eager
    mercy and make me new.

A Spinning Top

Do you remember the old-fashioned tops that could be started spinning by jerking a string that had been wrapped around them? Then there were those brightly painted metal ones that were started by pumping a handle in the middle; the more you pumped, the faster it turned.

The mystifying thing was that when someone gently touched the top as it was spinning, it suddenly danced away. It was as if there were something wrong about trying to hold it still. The faster the spinning, the quicker and more severe was the escape.

Is that the way it is with us, Lord? You reach for us because we are your own, but we are spinning through life at such a pace that we cannot be held. Even when the noise of life seems to diminish and our colors seem as one, you only need touch us and we jerk away. Our spin seems constant. Our thoughts propel us away from your efforts to hold us. We pump ourselves up, thinking this to be the way to "keep things going."

"Be still, and know that I am God."

No wonder we do not know more about you and about your knowing of us, Lord. We cannot be still.

Sometimes life bumps up hard against us. Our spinning comes to an abrupt halt. In those moments of tragedy, pain, or loss, we find that we can know you.

May we trust, O Lord, that we can lean our top quietly

against the table and wait for your hand to hold us.

Thank you for your patience, O One who set this top of ours spinning in space so long ago. Help us know that the source of our power is not always in the strong jerking of the string or in the hectic pumping of the handle. Power can also be found in being still in your hand.

Markings

There were only thin lines of struggle left as a traced memory of its last futile efforts. The paint had been wet, but the industrious spider had only its task etched in its mind. There had been no thought that the next steps might be into a shining trap that would grasp this builder of traps.

How many webs had this fuzzy-legged miniature of nature spun before it fell victim to man's glittering entrapment? How many unsuspecting bits of life had found their last moments held by this creature's woven bondage?

Now it, too, was held frozen in time, having left behind some distant web whose catch would be for some other. In the now dry paint were the tiny markings of its last desperate struggle, left for the living to read.

O Lord, sometimes we feel caught, trapped by what seemed so clear, so innocent. We are busy spinning our own webs as though we will always be around to maintain them. Someday you will read our markings as so much etching in the wet paint of life. May our marks not be just of struggle, but of joy, not just of having, but of giving.

And Lord, in that moment when life holds us fast, so much so that we shall not move again, may we know that only then shall we be fully caught in the marvelous web of your possessing love.

The Beat of a Different Drummer

He swayed back and forth, his fingers snapping in the air above his head. The rhythm that guided his movement came from beyond. Only he responded to the musical call, for its melody was trapped in tiny soft shells that filled his ears.

Whatever the impulse beating through those headphones, it compelled him to move. He was alone on a stereophonic carousel, swirling through a noisy world that he could not hear. The music was his master. He smiled in his servitude.

He was in that moment connected to the music. The melody resounded through his body, causing everything it touched to move. He was animated by some unseen spirit.

Put your earphones around my serious mind, O Lord, and fill me with the power of your harmony. Pace my slow step with the beat of your energetic love. Let me snap my fingers to the tune of your latest, upbeat creation. Then, after I have listened and taken off the headset, let me step off the carousel and walk out still singing your song into the noisy world.

Our Gods Die Hard

Our gods die hard:

- the god who controls everything so that life will turn out as we want and need it to;
- the god who is all smiles and whose judgment is like a replaceable part;
- the god who is all "mine" . . . all American . . . all Methodist;
- the god who is going to give me everything I want if I am good enough—the cosmic Santa Claus;
- the god who is at the beck and call of upper-middle-class folks but who remains distant from the poor and those who are oppressed;
- the god who is content to listen to individual concerns but who does not get involved in governments, systems, or institutions;
- the god who will never allow anything bad to happen to "me or my family."

These gods are quite mortal. They may die, for they are not God. They are our graven images created from our needs. They are golden calves, creations shaped from the melted-down fragments of our wishes. They are products of our effort to reverse the process of creation so that we make God in our image. As they die, the real God lives.

After the Storm

Snap—like the sound of a twig in a child's playful hand—that was the only sound it made. The fury of the wind and the rain covered up its crash to the ground. It was only after the skies cleared that I saw the huge tree lying across the side yard like a drowsy giant, not to be awakened.

Sudden grief came over me. My children had played in the branches of that tree; my wife and I had enjoyed its gift of shade on hot summer evenings. Even the squirrels seemed puzzled as one of their number surveyed the the once tall branches, now fallen.

How could nature contrive to steal my evergreen friend? Was the storm some kind of battle between forces to see who could survive? Was the wind smiling at its victory? Did the last bit of rain dance as it fell upon the once proud branches?

Often the mystery remains and the questions are left unanswered, but this time the reason for the downfall was exposed by the morning sun. Deep within the rich pulp of the tree's main branch was the darkness of disease. What looked so alive and strong on the outside was weak and dying on the inside.

You know our hidden weaknesses, do you not, Lord? Though we seem to stand tall, you know the flaws within that could, if tested too much, cause us to snap and become yet another casualty of life's constant weathering.

Goodbye, my evergreen friend. Thanks for the memories and for the reminder.

A Prayer for an Ordinary Day

It is just one of those ordinary days, Lord. It is no one's birthday that I know. There are no special events planned, no major problems to be faced—just another day.

But on a day much like today, shepherds made their way back to business as usual after greeting a new king born in a stable. The sun came up just like it did today that morning a weeping Mary asked her question: "Where have you taken my Lord?"

Somewhere today a woman struggles to give birth to life, an old man closes his eyes never to see this side of life again, and a boy tightens a rubber binding around his arm and injects a soft melted substance into his arm to shield him from the hard reality of life.

Today, around the corner from some galaxy we have yet to discover, a new star is born at the same moment that another one millions of light years away dies. On this day that I mark as ordinary, light from both of them participates in the creation of the shadow made on my sidewalk.

O Lord, thank you for this ordinary day, where all around me life explodes, leaving me quite still. I could not contain all that is happening on this day, and tomorrow my cup might run over with joy or sadness. So may I step gently into this day, remembering how awesome the ordinary can be.

School-Age Anxieties

I can remember the anxiety. What kind of year would it be? Whom would I have to sit beside? Would my teacher like me? Would I like him or her? Would math ever get any easier?

No one ever really talked about the fear at the beginning of a new school year. That was not done.

Those school-age anxieties and fears seem so simple now when seen in the light of the adult world. Childhood was so short-lived. Once in a while I wish I could sneak back there and worry only about memorizing my "eights." How nice it would be to sneak up behind Pat again and pull her braided ponytail.

Lord, bless our children as they begin a new school year. May their anxieties be no larger than they should be. May their minds be imprinted not only with knowledge but also with seeds of insight. May their teachers be allowed to see the good in them amidst the laughter and the pulling of ponytails.

And Lord, when as a grown-up I become entrapped in too much worry, help me pause a moment and remember those simpler days . . . and smile while practicing my "eights."

Distant Power

Foolish creature, running across the narrow bridge of wire as though it were just another branch on some tree. In its haste it does not realize that beneath its busy feet there runs enough power to not only provide energy for all the homes along my street but also to extinguish its tiny life if one wrong step is made.

Squirrels on a power line—an early morning parable of life. Are we not like them? We hurry through life not realizing the energy and power that is all around us. Because we have some task to accomplish, we are too preoccupied to experience the awe and wonder of life.

We expect that the line upon which we travel will always be there, leading to some other post which will be another jumping-off place for yet another task. What if we stopped to feel for a moment the power of life beneath our feet? In that pause we could sense that there is something larger and more full of energy than the busyness of our pace.

Would we not be more aware that life's steps should be taken with greater care, for hurried journeys can lead to destructive ends. The surge of life comes from a distant source we cannot see, and yet, it is beneath our feet and all around us. Look around and watch your step; life is full of wonder and power.

Christmas Cactus

The Christmas cactus in my office has decided to bloom. Just when Christmas had become but a distant memory and winter's harsh reality had put an end to "visions of sugarplums," out pops Christmas again. Does my cactus not know that we are through with Christmas? Childlike dreams and feelings have been put away to make room for the seriousness of enduring the frigid months ahead.

What are these springlike blooms to mean now? Perhaps they would have been appropriate during yuletide when so many artificially prompted poinsettias were alive with color. The colors of my cactus seem to know no time.

I suppose Jesus would enjoy sitting me down and using the opportunity of this late-blooming plant to tell a parable. At the appointed time, God's flower bloomed in our desert.

Just as my cactus does not follow a calendar, so God's inbreaking into life does not coincide with our celebrations. Maybe the cactus knew better than I that I would need a little Christmas color in late January.

Look around. Maybe something is trying to bloom in your winter. Better yet, perhaps you could be that surprise burst of color to someone else's bleak midwinter.

Letting Go

Change is a part of life, so they say. Why is it, then, that change is often scary and many times resisted? We creatures who like certainty seem to cling to our security and status quo. There comes a time, however, when we feel that change is good for us. Something deep within us calls for it. Perhaps it is our kinship with nature. The fall of the year makes it crystal clear that change is an intricate part of the cycle of life. The trees' beauty is a secondary element for what is primary—their need for change in order to live. Can you not just hear a maple tree's internal dialogue with its branches:

> But I like this year's shade of green. Why mess with something that is so cool and comforting? Besides, I know what comes after the fleeting color show—nakedness. I'm going to stay like I am this year!

We talk like this to ourselves because our roots run deep and we know the harshness of life's winds blowing through the empty spaces of our lives. Maybe this is the reason that our God makes autumn so colorful if but for a moment. The rainbow of change is a parable to us that there is hope within the seasons of our lives and that some change is essential for a full life.

I suppose that some years it comes natural for the maple to let go, but then there are other times when I have noticed one that seems to still be green when all around are bare.

Help us to let go when we need to, Lord. It just may add color to our lives.

Billie's Reminder

"What did you do with the sticker that the minister gave you during the children's sermon last week?" his mom asked. "What minister?" the three-year-old responded. "That was God!"

My wife and I laughed together as she recounted this incident. This called to my attention the rather surprising assertion made by Jesus that it is as children that we truly find the kingdom of God. Children have a way of breaking life open so that all the "stuff" of life spills out all over the floor. As we pick up the pieces, laughing or crying, some new truth usually becomes obvious.

So a child thought I was God; silly . . . perhaps not. Most of us have a hard time touching God. We do know, however, the reality of a human touch. We know how warm and healing that touch can be. We often have a hard time talking to God, but we remember how restoring the listening of one who cares can be.

In the loneliness that each of us feels at some time or another, we yearn for God's arms around us. Yes, Billie, I have been God to some people, just as you have helped me see God more clearly through your childish vision. We are called to put our arms around one another and be a part of God to others.

We are God's reality, the finest handiwork from God's shop—God's very image. God is much bigger than we are, but we are not so small that we cannot be an extension of divine love to one who needs God and us.

What was God's method for reconciling humankind? God sent a person to do it! And God sends us, too. We are God's people. We need to accept God's choosing of us because in certain moments we are the only part of God that someone may be able to touch, feel, or see.

Thanks, Billie, for the reminder.

Threads in the Fabric

Our story tells us that "in the beginning" God worked with all of creation to weave a tapestry. What God ended up with did not fit the intended design at all. It is hard to make a pretty picture from the Cain and Abel episode, the Tower of Babel, and a disastrous flood. God's tapestry seemed a mess from the very beginning.

Then the divine strategy changed direction. God decided to get specific instead of working with the general picture. A rather tired, old nomad named Abram was chosen, and he and his descendants were promised that they would be a chosen people. Those chosen people were then supposed to shine as a light for the nations and be an example of what God thought the picture ought to look like.

Remembering the story, we know that God's chosen folks tried to weave all sorts of threads of their own into the original design. They ended up tied in knots. There was the slavery in Egypt, the rise and fall of kingdoms, the exile by the waters of Babylon, and finally the occupation by the ruling power of Rome.

God may have thought a minute about the possibility of cutting the threads from the loom and starting over! Instead, God wove the finest thread right into the middle of the mess. It was God's last thread of hope, and it was about as specific as God could get. Folks tossed the finished product onto a garbage heap outside Jerusalem and buried the remains in a tomb.

God then had to pull out some threads so that we could see a picture in the midst of the torn tapestry. God, the Mender, then patched the tear with something we call resurrection.

There is only one other way God can be more specific in this weaving. God can use us to bring order out of chaos. The loom's shuttle can be heard weaving the pattern. We are part of the fabric that holds the whole thing together.

Psalms

The book of Psalms is a collection of personal yearnings shared with God. They contain words of praise, complaint, cries for vengeance, and portrayals of sufferings. Try writing your own psalm. Read some of the psalms and pick up your pen. Here's one I wrote:

O God, sometimes I feel your terrible absence.
I become afraid like a child who sees shadows in
     the dark
and runs to the window to find nothing.

Yet in my fear there is a stillness, a whisper of a
     voice.
I remember that even those times when I search for
     you and feel empty,
It is the longing for you, my God.

Great is my need for you, O God.
I am incomplete without you.
Teach me that even the times of emptiness
     are but the shadows in the evening
Cast by the ever present light of your love.

Now it's your turn.

The Lost Church

It simply was not there. I ran by the place where it should have been two or three times. I began to sweat both from the heat and from frustration. My family and I had gone back to visit my grandmother who still lived in the town of my childhood. I went for my morning run, planning my route so that I would pass by my old church.

I knew that twelve years earlier when I had passed by, the church had been sold and transformed into a greenhouse and nursery. Somehow that did not seem so bad. At least nurture and growth were still the products of the old white framed structure that had gently supported my own process of development.

But now I could not find the building at all. Had it been torn down? Somehow I could feel that it was still there. I circled over and over again, looking at the new structures that had been built over that sacred place from my past.

In my mind I pictured that older gentleman who used to rise and pray on those sultry Sunday evenings as we fanned away the humidity with the help of those paper fans with the face of a somber Jesus on one side and the funeral home advertisement on the other. I remembered seeing the joy on my grandmother's face as she sang those old hymns.

I did not mind the church being transformed into a plant nursery, for I was planted there myself in the rich soil of old-time religion. I had gone through many transplant shocks since those childhood days, but I still held a special place for those loving hands that first started me growing.

As I wiped the moisture from my face with my shirt, I saw it. In the middle of a newer structure there was the roof of the old sanctuary. It had been surrounded by yet another building. It had become a furniture store.

Much has been added to my frame of experience since those days of simple fan-cooled religion, but somewhere, hidden beneath the new, is that church of my beginnings. It will always be there, no matter what later construction covers it.

Necessary Pain

My youngest daughter's eyes were brimming with tears. She worked the tooth back and forth with her fingers. Her reward was in her grasp. It was up to her. Was the pain worth it? She could blame no one else. The pain came from her own decision.

I looked into her moist eyes. There was wavering determination hemmed with a slight thread of fear and anticipation. I was helpless—simply a bystander witnessing one of the passing miracles and lessons of growth.

For agonizing moments she continued her efforts. In the instant that my aged perception decided that defeat would be the victor, she screamed with excitement, "I got it!"

She went bounding into the next room to show her mother the prize. In her proud clutch was the tooth. For her efforts she would be visited by that magical childhood tooth fairy, whose job it is to whisk away the memories of the pain and replace them with materialistic rewards.

Joy followed her from room to room as she proclaimed her victory to all. The excitement brought a smile to my face and to my heart—such a lesson of life.

Growth involves necessary pain as the old must give way for the coming of the new. So many choices are in our hands. We can wait for time to do its work, or we can take hold and live through some sacrifice in order to allow for some slight death to make way for new life. It is not easy, this making way for the new. Tears are a part of growth. But what joy awaits us beyond the hesitation and the fear!

O Lord, how children do teach us. We have learned to avoid risk. We become timid in our growth. Help us to engage life so that after the needed struggle we can put some of our fear under the pillow and awake to the grace and laughter of existence.

Behind the Corners of Our Souls

It is amazing how the old demons never really die. They just seem to hide behind the corners of our souls and wait for moments of vulnerability, when our lives are torn open. Then they know that, even if uninvited, they can slip into the center of who we are, gnawing away at us because· they want us for themselves.

The demons know that if they consume enough of us, we will become like them. Then, as in some late-night vampire movie, our only choice becomes living at someone else's expense. Rather than drawing our life from the spirit within us, we must then gain our worth by overcoming someone else.

The demons are deceptively comely in their many disguises. The vision of them is usually quite appealing. It is the consequences of evil that are ugly; the entrapment itself is often quite beautiful.

The demons know our names. They are quite personal in the way they work. They become very close to us and offer us their subtle friendship. They want a home, because ever since God interfered, they have been homeless. They have no place that is their own. Their place was taken from them by a power that is greater than their own.

For now, they roam and wait patiently, learning. It would be comforting to think that they are not real, that they are really some childhood bogeyman whom we could outgrow. But they are real, and they do know our names. We must do battle with them especially in moments of our weaknesses, when we are so open to their entry into our lives.

We must recognize them for who they are and do as one of long ago did who conquered them. We must call them by name. As we name them, we gain power over them. We regain control of our lives so that we can choose to whom we shall give ourselves.

What are your demons' names . . . jealousy, envy, lust, power, unbridled success, blind selfishness, idle gossip, unwillingness to forgive, no vision for beauty? Name yours.

Running into the Mystery

I knew how beautiful the other side of the lake was, but I could not see it. The early morning fog held everything in its grasp. I was alone in the damp mystery that limited my vision; or was I?

Perhaps some other early morning runner was just ahead of me, running into the mystery. So often when we think we are alone, we are not.

Soon the sun appeared and dispersed what seemed to be the blanket that covered earth's morning bed. With the stretching creation came a bird's song to remind sleepy pilgrims that it was time to begin the day.

Burn it off, Lord, the fog that encloses me,
That I may see not only the path
But also those who travel with me.

May I trust that when the vision is hidden,
That still the truth is there,
Waiting for the veil to be folded back.

I will run into the mystery
And not be surprised when other steps are heard;
For many seek who cannot see,
And trust the sun to do the rest.

An Angel's Whisper

Over my shoulder I could hear the whisper: "It's really something, isn't it?"

I looked to discover the source of the message but was only greeted by the late afternoon breeze as it played with the branches of the nearby cedar. This particular afternoon was almost mystical in its beauty. The grass had become intense in its color, as though a child had been given the freedom to use all the crayons available for the picture.

The word "spring" is not big enough to contain all that was present that day. Winter's grip was fast becoming a fading memory as I observed creation's miracle from my porch swing. The swing became a place of magic as it moved me through the whispers of morning dampness or evening benedictions.

Then I heard it again: "Such beauty . . . and you had nothing to do with it. It is simply given to you as a gift. Gosh, what a day."

Still I could see nothing as I scanned the outline of the afternoon picture. Then I saw the light sifting through its wings as it jumped across the breeze. It came to rest on the vine that wove through the spaces of the wrought iron.

Could it be that on its journey across spring this winged marvel with such beautiful markings wanted to share something with another one of earth's creatures? To it I must have appeared strange indeed, perched on a porch swing.

The butterfly paused but for a moment as though taking one last look at me. Then it was lost in the tapestry of green.

In the midst of video recorders and tax returns, bills to pay and persons battling illness, sounds of headlines echoing the news of terrorist's attacks . . . came a message: "It's really something, isn't it?"—an angel of spring bearing the message of creation's gift.

Resurrection Song

What is this summer bloom,
   inappropriate to nature's seasons?
Last year's Easter lily,
   buried in earth's warm tomb,
     has awakened to June's morning.

It is awkward in its beauty,
   for its time is earlier,
And its setting one of potted soil and stained-glass
   windows;
   its rest near some empty cross.

The red of the geranium flushes with embarrassment
   at the intruder.
"It is not Easter," whispers the sturdy fern.
   And the monkey grass simply laughs at the sight.

Bothered not by the noise,
   the white trumpets sound of Easter.
Released from the grave clothes of artificial birthing
   in glass houses,
   they play a resurrection song.

Then other blooms grow silent
   as the Creator again shows
That resurrection is in God's hand
   and not bound in some calendar of days;
So God smiles while Easter comes in June.

Struggling Life

He pulled his fabric suitcase out of the car. His thin frame carried it lightly, indicating that its contents must have been slight. A blue tam-o'-shanter covered his head. Beneath the woolen cap was a face narrow and drawn. His cheekbones told the story of past days of treatments. As I followed him down the hospital corridor, I saw him turn to go through a set of doors that led to the oncology unit. The cap surely covered a head whose hair had fallen victim to the efforts of healing.

Walking before me was life struggling with life. I wondered why he was alone this day. Was it by choice, or were the ones who were part of his story in years past now hiding in the background, afraid?

Was he coming back for more treatments with a sense of hope, or was his suitcase the only light thing about his life on this day? Did he have someone with whom to share his fear, his dreams, perhaps even his death? Would there be a happy ending, or would the fabric suitcase be sold at some yard sale with no one knowing its story?

The autumn wind greeted me as I left the hospital. The wind's message was full of colored leaves, telling me of life and death in the same moment. How much we need to listen to the swirling stories all around us. Our days are full of people we do not see or hear.

I stopped in the parking lot and allowed the leaves to blow over my feet. I listened for a moment to the beating of my own heart. The wind told me of lives too full and suitcases too empty.

Desperate Lunges

Freedom seemed so clear. The sparrow flew toward the rays of sunlight, but twice it threw itself against the garage window. I had startled it as I opened the door to go into the basement of my home. Fear compelled the bird to seek the quickest escape. But what looked to be a passage of light was just a reflection framed by a window.

I stood frozen, not wanting to panic the frightened creature any more than I already had. Still it vainly attempted its escape. Behind me was the opening to the garage, waiting for the bird. All it needed to do was turn in the direction of its fear and fly over my shoulder.

The sparrow perched on an old table, pondered its options, felt its pain, and suddenly flew past me into the warm light of spring. It did not fly far, but settled just outside the garage as if to look back at what had happened.

Are we like that bird, Lord? We struggle to escape through what seems like easy freedom. We learn slowly, sometimes only because of our pain. Our fears keep us from seeking the real path of freedom.

Do you stand by and watch our desperate lunges, wanting us to choose a less painful way? You startle us occasionally when we find you, for we think you are far away. We are afraid. Help us to trust that we will only find real freedom in the flight toward you.

Seasons of the Gospel

Into the Night

She felt the life within her move. Fear held her
mind even as joy possessed her heart. Why should she
doubt the voice of God? What was it that moved
within her alongside the gentle pushing of a child
stretching its arms? Uncertainty should not be a part
of her soul's wonderings.

So much was beyond her ability to believe. Even as
two hearts now beat within her, she felt torn between
allowing her thoughts to dance among the stars of the
clear evenings and pondering the unreality of being
chosen as the mother of God's ideas.

But what caused such uneasiness just now was the
recent news that she would have to accompany her
betrothed on a journey to comply with the wishes of a
government that surely must be the product of evil.
Could this be if God were truly at work within her?

The journey would be hard, but she could not be
without her Joseph, the one who had stood with her
in the midst of all the whispers and possible shame.
Now she could not bear the solitude. She would go
with him to Bethlehem and trust that somehow God
knew what he was doing.

Joseph helped her up onto the burro, that same
gentle beast who had so many times carried timbers to
his shop. Mary let her fingers run tenderly along the
brow of her bearer. She reached for Joseph's
calloused hand and placed it upon her swollen
stomach. Mary smiled as she looked at Joseph's hand

resting on her body. She could tell by his expression that he had felt the child leap also. In this they were together, though all alone. The only other that felt such movement that night was God.

Into the fear, into the night, they left for Bethlehem . . . .

Lost in Bethlehem

Darrell's eyes were full of innocent wonder. He kept time to the Christmas carols by swinging back and forth in his rocking chair. Once in a while his eyes closed and he seemed to be wandering in some "silent night" or perhaps roaming for himself down the narrow streets of that "little town of Bethlehem."

Each year I looked forward to going to Darrell's house before Christmas. His home was always the last stop on our youth group's annual caroling venture.

The first few years I felt sorry for Darrell, especially when he cried when we sang "Silent Night." He experienced Christmas and the rest of his life as a child, for Darrell was a person with mental retardation.

Even when I became an adult and lived miles away, I always returned to my home church so that I could go caroling. Life was becoming serious, and Christmas was losing its magic. Darrell's smiles, his rhythmic rocking chair, and his silent tears helped me remember something beyond all the words I kept hearing about the meaning of Christmas.

I no longer felt sympathy for Darrell. The tears that blurred my vision that last time I sang in his home were shed more for me than for him. Somehow I knew that he was closer to the manger than I would ever be. On that still night, for a moment, I roamed the busy streets of Bethlehem with Darrell.

Oh to be so lost again . . . .

Christmas Drama

The angels squirmed nervously in their seats. The shepherds peered around their teacher, who stood in the doorway attempting to keep them from entering the scene too early. The children were more like eager sheep than dutiful shepherds.

Mary and Joseph sat anxiously yet symmetrically beside the manger, awaiting the moment when they would become instant stars because of "the" star, which in this scene, hung shimmering from the chancel cross at the back of the sanctuary.

Parents' faces broke into smiles, some so joyous there were almost tears. Children arrayed in costumes representing everything from teddy bears to wise men popped up like living jack-in-the-boxes to say well-memorized one liners.

Did anyone in the packed sanctuary that night of the children's Christmas program understand the "true" meaning of Christmas? Did I?

I looked at Mary and Joseph perched on their stools as if ready for a race, ready for that moment when, suddenly, Mary would jump from her stool and grab baby Jesus. Joseph would obediently stand beside her, swaying a little back and forth to the tune of heavenly hosts. They were well trained.

The shepherds made their long-awaited entrance, much to the pleasure of a fatigued doorkeeper. The wise men brought their gifts, which strangely resembled foil-wrapped margarine containers, and laid them before a smiling Mary and Joseph.

What "is" the real meaning of Christmas? Who knows? Joy to the world . . . let heaven and nature sing. Let nervous shepherds bounce. Let excited angels squirm. Let teddy bears come to life and sing off key.

What is the real meaning of Christmas? A star hangs from a cross; light comes to a dark world. The crooked way shall be made straight. The desert shall bloom . . . and teddy bears will come to life.

Putting Away the Babe

You still smile at me,
  though I pack you away.
Your reaching hands grasp darkness
  as I close the box that holds you.

Shall you dream until next season when I set you
    free?
Or do you weep, for the time was short that you
    graced my mantle.

Would your hands rather reach into all the light of
    my days
And rest quietly as I dream through all the nights of
    the year?

O infant Jesus that manger held,
  how easily you are put away.
For we can abide you for but a time,
  And then we must return to life as is.

So I shall wrap you gently,
  entombing you for yet another year.
But bindings shall not keep you,
  for Easter light on Christmas shines,
And as you reach into my darkness,
  only your smile is there.
for you are free!

Scholars, Dreamers, or Kings?

History calls us kings, but we were no different from countless others who have looked to the stars and longed for meaning. We had studied more than some, that is true, for our sacred texts told of one who was to come who would be a king like no other king.

The movement of the stars matched the journey of our hearts, so we left our homes and took the pilgrimage. After lengthy deliberations, we departed in silence, for we knew not where the stars would lead us.

At different times and at various places along the way, each of us voiced doubts about what we were doing. As the many evenings dimmed and our journey grew longer, our hopes began to diminish. Perhaps we were dreamers rather than scholars.

Our charts seemed to tease us. No one we encountered on our journey seemed to be looking for any new king. Then came the star splitting the darkness on that very evening when the darkness seemed so deep.

The longer our journey had grown the more each of us had come to realize that our destination would hold something unexpected; but when we knelt beside the cattle trough and presented our gifts, we were surprised by our complete awe and reverence.

Beside his manger, in the light of his star, perhaps we were kings.

God's Fireworks

"Epiphany"—a funny sounding word. It sounds like something one should stumble across while playing *Trivial Pursuit.* The card might read, "What is an epiphany?"; and the expected answer might be, "the lower left metatarsal bone of an aardvark."

Our not-so-trivial pursuit of the meaning of "epiphany" tells us something quite clear. It is as plain as the smile on your face, as clear as a winter's night illumined by an unusually bright star. Epiphany is God's "coming out" party, the announcement of God's engagement with the world.

Epiphany simply means "manifestation," but that is too simple. It is God's fireworks, for while Christmas may have been quiet and simple, epiphany is about as loud as God gets.

Epiphany is the world halting at a manger, represented by wise men who came from distant lands. Epiphany is an old man named Simeon hanging around the temple, unable to die until he holds God's son in his hands. Epiphany is that same grey-haired man holding the infant Jesus up in his outstretched arms and shouting, "Now let thy servant depart in peace because I have seen thy salvation." Epiphany is the celebration of Jesus' own baptism day when the proud father said to the soaking wet son, "I am so proud of you" or, better translated, "This is my beloved Son in whom I am well pleased."

"Epiphany"—that funny sounding word that we

need more than ever as we walk away from the manger. We all need some manifestation in a world where wisdom seems overshadowed by the bright-shining star of technology. We need the assurance that, like the about-to-give-up Simeon, we can hold salvation in our reach.

Epiphany reminds us of the voice that whispered in our ears at our baptisms saying, "You, too, are one of my own children in whom I am well pleased."

The Arrival

Gnats flew patterns around his matted beard. The desert sweat left trails of salt which disappeared into his hairy face. He was tired but full of fire. His weariness stemmed not from the draining heat of the Judean sun, but from the growing burden he carried. His words weighed him down.

He called the Pharisees snakes and shouted to them that their white robes could not hide their slithering deceit. His arid voice caught the attention of Herod when the foul-smelling desert prophet pronounced his sentence upon the king: crown or no crown, adultery was adultery.

John's voice was indeed in the wilderness, and his solitude grew deeper, even as the seeking crowds came to him to be baptized. The dryness in his mouth could not be quenched even with the water he used to give the people hope. It was the fire in his words that left him longing for the dampness of a salvation he seemed unable to provide. So many eyes were looking to him for answers and for light in the growing darkness of a world that often seemed to be forgotten by God.

John could give them water and the promise of forgiveness, but he could not give them what he, too, sought. The longing in the wet faces of those he brought up out of the waters asked him if he was the one for whom they waited.

He tried to hide his own disappointment at not

finding the Messiah among the people. He shouted all the more the promise so as to convince even himself.

His mind wandered somewhere far away into the desert, though his body was waist deep in the slowly-moving flow of the Jordan. At first he did not even see the pilgrim who knelt before him in the river waiting to be baptized. But then he caught the sunlight reflecting from the beads of sweat on the man's face and recognized him.

"I need to be baptized by you, and do you come to me?" he managed to speak.

In the background there was thunder, and a white dove dipped down near them in its sweeping flight. Still dripping with the water of John's baptism, the pilgrim walked toward the desert, leaving behind the solitary prophet drowning with joy. He was here! John splashed water onto his own face as one who had finished a long journey. For the first time in many months he felt his thirst satisfied.

Dusty Fingers

"From dust you came and unto dust you shall return" were the words I used as I made the sign of the cross on the foreheads of those who knelt at the altar on Ash Wednesday. The words were as dark as the ashes that now marked the few who had made their way to this inauguration of the Lenten season. After all, who wants to be reminded that they are dust and that one day they will become part of that which they kick up every day under foot?

I looked at my blackened fingers. The more I tried to wipe away the dust, the more it spread across my other fingers. The ashes were not going to let me forget. I could not escape the memory of my mortality. The more I tried to disperse the dust, the more I was reminded.

As I washed my hands and wiped my forehead clean later that evening, I remembered the promise: "He will wipe away every tear . . . and death shall be no more" (Revelation 21:4).

To live is to be stained with mortality. To live is to make ashes of promises made by us and not kept. To live is to pretend that we are not dust . . . but we are. The only way we will be able to wipe the stuff from our fingers is with the help of the One who in the beginning shaped the dust and breathed life into it.

Lent is an abrupt reminder that we are of the earth. Lent, however, is also the beginning of the promise that death is but the wiping away of the dust from our lives.

. . . And he walked out of the tomb, shook off the dust, and spoke to us of life.

The New Covenant

They noticed that his hands trembled slightly as he lifted the cup for the blessing. It was a surprising moment, for he had been so sure and strong before. Perhaps he was tired, exhausted from the thrills of a parade, of sorts, held in his honor, worn thin by his skirmishes with the religious leaders over the past weeks.

He seemed far away as he lifted the cup above their heads. His eyes looked up as he said the words of thanksgiving, words offered by countless people before this night. His eyes returned to them and it was as if he had been on a distant journey. He smiled and passed the cup to John with words that were new, not traditional: "Drink this, for this is my blood shed for you. It is the cup of the new covenant."

Peter wondered, *What new covenant?* Matthew pondered the cost. Thomas speculated over just what would be new about it. James and John began a hushed debate over which of them truly understood the newness. Judas thought to himself how it was now too late for anything new.

Then there was a sudden silence as they noticed Jesus looking pensively at his hands, hands that after a moment reached for one of the loaves in the basket. He broke the loaf slowly. The blessing this time was spoken so quietly that it almost was not heard. The words he spoke after the blessing, however, they would not forget: "Take, eat, this is my body broken for you."

Today we call it Eucharist, which means "thanksgiving." Only later, though, would those first disciples share in the thanksgiving, for that evening they were lost amidst unanswered questions.

A Soldier's Story

God, I wish this was over. This garment I won is small payment for this evening's agony. Perhaps it can at least keep the damp night air off my shoulders.

I wonder how long he had it draped over his back before it was stripped from him. I wish my zealous partners had not thrown it back over his blood-covered body so soon after they had beaten him. Now these stains spoil the little bit of beauty the robe possessed.

The wretch who now hangs on the cross gambled and lost. I gambled for his cloak and won. What a fool he must be to allow himself to be trapped by powers bigger than himself. He should have worried more about the garment on his back and less about whatever cause it was that put him on a cross.

I overheard my fellow soldiers laughing after I had won the game that brought me this cloak. They were asking the pathetic king where his subjects were now. I suppose I have hanging over my shoulders his princely mantle. Perhaps I should ask him from what kingdom my souvenir comes.

It matters not. This crucified king is not long for this world. He seems to be dying more quickly than most. The beatings must have been more severe than usual. We have learned to hate these Jews. After all, they are the reason we are in this God-forsaken desert of a land.

At least for this forgotten king, tomorrow will not

bring any more pain. I grow tired of the causes and the religion that seem to provide constant tension among these strange people.

What kind of people are they who want their kings crucified? It is a shame about these blood stains. I wonder if soaking it would help. Well, king, I will keep your blood-soaked tunic as something to remember your fallen kingdom by; it will be all that is left of your reign.

Wounded Hands

Hands that reached and touched so many;
Now bound to a cross, unable to touch.
Untouchable hands, unreachable love
  reaching the untouchable.

Friday's shadow spreads over places where no light
    has been.
Even those who do not want this scene are now
    touched.
No escaping this once unreachable touch
  now brought close.

Motionless hands unmovable, bound by nails and
    love.
How quiet he is, never to touch again;
  unreachable forever.
Hands folded in the posture of death;
  unreaching, entombed.

Unthinkable it is, his hands reaching;
  touching again!
Freshly scarred hands unbound,
  touching Death to make it alive.
Hands that reached and touched so many,
  touch me.

Forget

He looked out from his balcony.
The cool night air clung to him like dew on the grass
   waiting for the morning sun.
At least it was over;
  Each one could now go back to his chosen
  obsession.

As for him, he was tired of all the fanatic squabbling
   of recent days.
He would never understand these people who were
   compelled to answer to him.
Their hate for him was clear, but why this disgust for
   one of their own?

He found the man to be quite innocent,
  except for the crime of honesty.
Well he knew what condemnation that brought.
So the man was a foolish idealist;
  No reason to slaughter him for grasping at dreams.

They were a pathetic people,
  worshiping a god who had long deserted them.
This betrayed leader said he offered them a new
   kingdom
  in the midst of despair.
But those who held tightly to their little power were
   afraid,
  and fear can destroy.

"But they had to use me to rid themselves of his
    cause
  that seemed to spread.
Powerless, they screamed for strange justice.
What was he to me?
  And yet, never have I seen such a look.
He was more foolish than they in his death.

"And now the night air brings rumors of his limp
    escape from the tomb;
Carried off by friend or angry foe?
Can they not at least leave him now?
  They need do as I have done;
  Wash their hands and forget.
Tomorrow's sunrise and his name will be lost amidst
    some new fear."

  Pilate turned and walked toward his bed and tried
    again to sleep.

Creation Held Its Breath

Creation held its breath;
Shades of this mystery had been seen before.
Did the seed not die for the blossom of tomorrow?

But was not dust only the cradle,
   That which held the possibility of the new from the old?
Could the dust which held his breath breathe again?

The trees had heard his cry;
   For sleepy disciples lay dreaming beneath their
      branches.
Only the trees heard his plea to take away the cup.

The earth felt the warmth,
   His blood falling from a cross to the waiting soil.
Like rain from heaven,
   the earth treasured this life.

The rock sheltered his limp body,
   A final rest after a long journey through so many lives.
"Sleep," whispered the rock of the tomb.
   "My silence shall not disturb you."

As creation held its breath,
   the thunder broke open the morning.
Precious dust was filled again with life.
The trees, the earth, the rock welcomed him.
   He was alive again.

"I Must See"

"I for myself must know that it's true;
  My eyes must know what is real.
His hands, his feet, his very wounds,
  I must see and touch and feel.

"And now you tell me you have seen
  What my heart longs to be so.
But simple words will not suffice;
  This time I have to know.

"For the nights will be empty without him,
  His message needs strength to remain.
I cannot rely on your witness.
  His wounds, he must now explain.

"How can we offer to others,
  What we in fact question to be?
I must have the truth of the matter,
  No more babbling, for now I must see."

Then Thomas felt light in his darkness,
  And the shadows were gone from the room.
Before him was the one who had called him,
  The one they had placed in the tomb.

"Well, Thomas, you wanted to see me;
  To believe you just had to know.
But many will never be certain,
  And believe just because it is so.

"So, Thomas, reach out and touch me
  For those who will never achieve
Such a touch as you now render
  But in spite of will say, 'I believe!' "

On the Road Again

Let us go, Cleopas, to a place away from the crying.
I am tired of breathing the heavy air of pain.
Travel with me to Emmaus and help me to forget.

He should have done it differently, having known
      better.
It is almost as if he chose the way of a cross.
That way is steep and foolish and . . . Emmaus is not
      far now.

It is of no use convincing this stranger who
      understands not.
He would have had to be there to feel the
      disappointment.
How interesting of him to appeal to old
      prophets—nothing new.

Let us stop, Cleopas; you, too, stranger.
      My mind is weary with words.
Perhaps some food will fill the emptiness made deeper
      by this stranger.
I remember once our Lord spoke of having no need
      for bread, but as for me . . .

O nameless friend, would you ask the blessing, we are
      tired.
You seem to have reverence for our laws.
      Uphold us with their words.
Our laws grow tasteless in our mouths,
      so bless our bread.

Cleopas, his hands, more fresh than the loaf, with
    wounds.
Life's grain sown in our midst while we were
    sleepwalking.
Lord, stay . . . but you will not. Cleopas, let us go
    back.

Peter Remembers

The fire cooked the fish,
Freshly caught from a sea
  He once tamed with
    but a few words.

    There he was, simply preparing
Food for us like some servant;
  On his knees again as on
    the night of the foot washing.

    So common was his wonder,
That he would never be the king
  we so wished him to be.
  A king frying fish!

    He must have known we would
Soon return to the familiar boats,
  So he again prepared to feed
    those who seemed so hungry.

    But he knew my emptiness came
Not from want of fish and bread.
  The knawing within came
    from a craving to deny my denial.

    Handing me fish, he told me
To feed his sheep and love him.
  Remembering that other meal of
    bread and wine, I said yes.

    Feed me, Lord, forever, for so
Meager is my love of you,
  But I shall go to my knees
    with towel and bread.

I have learned, Jesus, the
Power of your strange, weak ways.
And on my knees I cannot deny
I do know you,
my wounded king and Savior.

Divine Rest

Somewhere just beyond the stars,
  Doesn't God lay his tired head down gently upon
  the dusty Milky Way,
For He must be weary from dealing with a world
  whose weight seems heavier each day.

Surely he must close his eyes and enclose himself in
  some divine, serene darkness,
If but for a short nap, if not slumber,
  To keep himself from growing too weary as he
  holds up so much, so long.

The stars are silent as he draws breath deeply in the
  midst of rest,
For his ageless watch has its toll.
  He is such an old God, this one whose face is
  wrinkled with wisdom and love.

What a thought to imagine God sleeping;
  No surprise, for we feel his presence gone in
  moments of our own darkness.
But it is our need for rest we lay upon God,
  for he sleeps not, even in the longest night.

Only one time in all of light and love did he rest his
  head
And that was but for a cutting instant
  When his only offspring slept within a tomb.
God did then close his eyes for a moment.

"Never again," he spoke to the stars,
  "Will I rest in my watch of you."
And when his son arose,
  He peeled the death from around his brows
    and told us for all time,
      "God sleeps not."

Drunk Again!

"Give them the breathalizer! It's obvious that these guys have been up all night celebrating something."

That is what some of the crowd thought when they saw how Peter and the other disciples were acting on that day we call Pentecost. Peter had to walk the straight line and touch his finger to his nose blindfolded just to show the crowd that the spirit he was full of was not obtained the night before at the Jerusalem package store.

"Listen, folks, we're not drunk, just excited!" he told the laughing people in the street. They knew better, for many of them had seen how depressed these same disciples had been the last few weeks without the charismatic leadership of their ringleader. The preposterous story of his ascending into heaven made the people witnessing the disciples' strange babbling all the more sure that what they saw this particular morning was a group of people who had tried to drink their blues away.

Can you imagine being so excited about your faith, your church, your Lord, that someone would actually accuse you of being drunk? It is that season again—Pentecost. It is the season for us to remember that a group of depressed, lost followers turned the world upside down after they became "drunk" with the Spirit of God—a Spirit that danced around their upper room like tongues of fire.

Can the living spirit of our Lord add such

excitement to our rather ordinary faith? If we are going to be accused of something, at least let it be, "They're drunk again," rather than living out a faith that mildly resembles a hangover.

Dancing Tongues

Dull minds, sharpened by fire;
  Dancing tongues speaking to ears once filled with
  hope.

Excited followers, recently lost,
  Remembering sleepy nights in a garden while he
  prayed alone.

Windblown faces, facing uncertain futures,
  Feeling deserted by the one who promised them so
  much.

Sudden fire, heaven sent,
  Burning away binding memories,
    And in the ashes, Spirit's freedom.

Babbling disciples, filled with new wine,
  Not from some twisted vine;
    Sent from the wounded hands of God.

An empty room, still bathed with fire;
  Spirit-filled followers, no longer lost.
    Set free to scorch the earth with tongues of fire.